THE SECRET OF ARCHERY

THE SECRET OF ARCHERY

ALESSIO ZANELLI

Greenwich Exchange
London

Greenwich Exchange, London

First published in Great Britain in 2019
All rights reserved

Printed and bound by imprintdigital.com
Cover design by December Publications
Tel: 028 90286559

Author website: www.alessiozanelli.it

Greenwich Exchange website: www.greenex.co.uk

Cataloguing in Publication Data is available from the British Library

Cover art: courtesy of Shutterstock

ISBN: 978-1-910996-30-0

To Jane

Fundamentally the marksman aims at himself.

— Daisetsu Teitarō Suzuki

CONTENTS

LEAVE

Mizzle up the blue,
hills asleep in the haze,
rainbows fixed across the dale,
a watercolor sun afloat upon cloud-rags,
dry-stone walls and branches whistling in the gale –
pushing forward apace back home in the slanting liquid light
as the Westerlies blow the Old Year away.

A CRITIQUE OF FOG

The moral law is something Kant revealed in full,
by far the simplest rule to live consistent with.
But then what would Immanuel be induced to hold,
should he at last realize that *in* and *out* coincide,
a stubborn fog be all by which he's tensely bound,
and not a single star above his head be found?

ICEBLINK

Cold yellow, as of winter sun; even the silhouette of stocky white
mulberries – usually mighty and sharp – looks fuzzy, virtually

rubbed out by the glare. The air sizzles noiselessly, pervades
the outerwear, invades into the mouth, slips liquid down

the windpipe. And in front of the breadth, of the overflowing energy
of the glittering sweep, one would want to be the river – streaming

careless through it, not bothered at all, about still – subverter of
time and disrupter of space. One would nearly miss the uncolored

clouds – shapeless cover, border and detail swallower which
compacts everything, in so doing annulling it. One instinctively seeks

a mark, a scratch in the glow that brings back to time and reinstates
in space, a sheet anchor. So, between a row of skeletal poplars and the

water-grazing flight of crows, at last one yields to diffused light, harboring
the illusion of being able to gather and dominate it by reciting a line by

Tranströmer or humming a tune by Mussorgsky. For all one strives
to have a way with it, the glints can't be stolen from the enfolding range.

MISSING NEIGHBOR

He used to speak at length, all he possessed
enclosed within a cardboard box. No lamp
lit up the spot, he'd chosen well. Obsessed
with all he said about the outcast camp,
his lone retreat, I'm sure he'd tried his best.

I liked to call there every night to say
hello, till he was gone, his homestead bare,
a streetlight placed right where he always lay,
a lot of people hanging round the square.
I wish to think he simply moved away.

AQUANAUT

Water prison.

Inside the bubble still –
environed, sunken, missed.

Terra firma.

Who says it's out of reach?
The sky is gliding by.

Chances surface.

Whatever means will do –
a raft, a wreck, a whale.

A MIGRANT'S LAY

They'd said at least I would have had a chance.
It took me endless days, a slave again,
and sleepless nights, with past and future ghosts,
to save the cash and find the guts for it.
I'll always bless the time at last I quit.

No desert, thug or sickness could have me,
as long as my beloved child walked by,
until this long-awaited water did.
Already gone, I only let it win
when trawlers neared my girl and pulled her in.

THE PICTURE

On the sly, the hand into the drawer.
The one that should have never been pulled out.
Of a sudden, from under a dusty sheaf
of dated sepia postcards, the picture.
The one that should have never been retrieved.
A shiver down the spine,
a bitter smile, as twisted as fleeting,
for an instant the impulse to tear it,
as if the two gloating looks could be killed
by ripping to shreds the paper bearing them.
Afterwards long minutes,
the sunlight slowly fading in the room,
staring at those sneering faces,
supposed to speak
before being wrapped in darkness.
Maybe expecting both to say
what was wished to be heard
rather than the truth.

IN THE BATHROOM, READING AUDEN

In the bathroom, reading Auden,
envisioning marvelous pinnacles,
how not to fear unconquered peaks;
the eyes jumping among the rhymes
of affectionate *In Memory of W. B. Yeats*;
contemplating giants: of rock, of ice,
of powerful words one after another;
how cool to realize, as a mulish pacer,
I subdued both my muse and my ogre:
now they strive to follow in my wake.
I finally found my virgin Jomolungma
across finite but unbounded plains.
The two-coast elegist would nod.

TWONE
To dad

I hope for some more time before we'll have to part,
more looks, more words, and more of all I've always spared.

At times I feel so distant that there seems to be
no tie, no common past, no sharing blood or soul.

Though close, we may appear as perfect strangers but
no silence could conceal the truth: sheer likeness speaks.

I fear there'll be too much untold, unshown, passed by,
till I perceive how I am him and he is me.

It has been so since when – black-haired, strong-armed – he used
to lift and hold me up above, a tiny babe.

And now that spots and wrinkles grace his thinning face,
will I grow old in turn as brave to stand both weights?

THE HOURGLASS

Wheat fields. Amused-faced scarecrows. Breezy. Torrid. Bright.
Lines of mildly-swaying-topped black poplars. Tractors' and
threshers' engines' rumble. Lizards in and out the fissures.
Cicadas uninterruptedly chirping. Rapturous wonder.
Belonging. Careless running. Sweat and screams.
Out of breath. Laughter and tears. Adream.
The wish for the day to never end.
Achievement at twilight.
Sweet exhaustion.
Blissful
sleep.
Pictures
collected, carefully
arranged, crammed into a
fancied chest locked up and never
reopened. Like the real one filled up with
old clothes we have always lacked the courage to
discard or pass on as awkward hand-me-downs. Like
granddad's bulky retro leather case, abandoned in the loft
under a layer of dust, stuffed with keepsakes and postcards,
as well as exercise books a child today would hardly recognize.

THE PIN

I had been planning routes since I was born,
till someone moved the pin across the map.
My destination changed.
New paths had to be plotted.
I took all the time I needed
prior to setting off,
not a day too few and none too many.
Thence I became a tireless seeker.
Rotations followed countless.
And then revolutions.
On and on without a pause.
Onward-bound forever.
Nobody's moved the pin again.
Now the map is worn,
so are my shoes.
Its luster has long tarnished,
so has my dream.
The turning motions never stop,
and still I'm on my way.
The pin's awaiting finding.

CLIMBERS

Misty-footed further off, they cast their tops
up in the sky – gold slivers on lapis lazuli.
And yet they're wholes – there are no parts,
no discontinuities. They're huge and grand.
Young but primal, transcendent standers –
most pure and perfect absolutes. Monoliths.
Fixed out there for us to win or be won by.

There is no escape – we have to tackle them,
surmount their heads and possess that blue.
Yes, once come this far it's all we're left to do
to make things right. It'll take our best – then,
no hesitation. The solid sun of dawn has just
begun to smash against their summit walls.
We must be going, we must meet verticality.

Resplendent heights will not keep frozen long.

RETRIEVING PHYSIS

Ahead the wind will blow on end,
the thread rescind, the glow portend;

all shades and shrouds will fly apart,
parades of clouds thereby will dart.

And then the clock will stop to tick,
again the lock will flop and click;

we'll rove and run, so did Thoreau,
he strove and won, while we'd let go.

THE BOOK ABOUT TO BURN

On top of the campfire stack stands
a book, aged and worn, crumpled
pages aflutter in the wind, which
some absent-minded one forgot
right there or some reprobate
rejected. The wood's dry, ready
to give out good flames, as soon as
furtive hands deposit an ember at its
base. But not the book, not its thinned,
etiolated paper, hidden to light for
years, even longer to eye. All
that is written on it is not
ready to blaze, the
fleeting heat and glow
it would add to those from
the pile wouldn't be beneficial
to anybody. There's still plenty of
time to turn each word to ash, a
precise time, utterly apt. This
isn't the time for desperate
carelessness, impudent
depravedness, terrorized
groping in the dark, raped
identities. There's no book's
flame that may light our way.

HOW TO MAKE A PEBBLE MATTER

At the height of summer
look for pebbles underwater,
some fifty yards from the shoreline.

Pick up one you like,
choose the right angle
and throw it onto the sand,
then call it a date,
exactly the day on which the sea
will take it back as its own.

Remember:
the bigger the wave and flatter the strand,
the deeper the overlap;
the shallower the water, stronger the wind,
longer the blowing and further the fetch,
the bigger the wave;
the wind always does its part,
on both water and sand;
the pebble's shape, size and weight do matter;
no weather forecast ever is of any help.

The rules:
you may have one go;
if your throw can't reach the beach,
you can't play this game;
if you make an accurate guess,
you win;
if the sea takes the pebble sooner than you said,
the sea wins;
if the sea doesn't take the pebble by the end of the day you said,
nobody wins and you may play again next year.

Lastly:
if someone else collects the pebble sooner than the sea,
the pebble wins.

THE WALK

The spool's unwound,
the thread unwoven,
the weaver's hands worn out,
the loom long frozen.

What's left is just a road,
the one of a novel kind.
Weaving turns to walking,
non-spaced, non-timed.

The walk leads nowhere but to itself,
is not for usual flops,
takes more than simple years,
does not admit of stops.

THE INSOMNIACS

They don't sleep. They don't want to sleep.
The night has already gathered momentum –
they fear the stars may prove to be soothsayers.
The core of the Earth has long been cooling down.

They don't sleep. They can't sleep.
As if the birth of a brand new world
were just about to destroy the old one.
They do know the journey is shortening.

The horizon is drawing near,
the movement is winding down
while the crown is jammed forever.
It could well happen any moment now.

THE WITCH OF HEADS LANE

There's a huge stony Celtic harp on the driveway,
by which a stony hooded druidess sits and stares,
pensive over facing woody slopes in Ewden Valley.
The tiny house is made of blackened millstone grit
just like almost every structure on the moorlands,
but the weirdly elusive soul of her who lives in it
stands apart from all the people's in the milieu.
Céad míle fáilte reads a ground-fixed marble tile
in plain sight right at the entrance to the premises,
yet for sure nobody's feeling welcome once inside.
No one's ever seen the chimney smoking in winter,
any courageous beastie venturing the eerie yard,
any wild flower showing in the unattended garden.
There's a witch inhabiting a cottage up Heads Lane,
although most may think she simply exists as a fancy.
However, if you want to stroll the hill ridge – I daresay,
you'd better hurry past the place and not be peeking.
Before being hexed the Vicar used to live a mile away.

NIGHTCAP AT BOLSTERSTONE

Between the pitch-black outline of the hills
and the slate-indigo bank of stratocumuli
there is room for a band of clear sky,
ranging from citron yellow to cherry red
through hues of golden and orange.
The time to stop halfway along Stone Moor Road,
bend over the drystack wall fencing the lea,
feed half an apple each to the chestnut and the bay –
and the glow has thinned to a fiery slit.
Droplets start to beat on our cheeks aslant,
make us hurry upslope against the wind.
Inside the solemn-looking Castle Inn,
quite unkempt however almost empty,
just whispered chatting and subdued lighting,
as if they didn't want to attract attention.
Among them chaps there seems to be no regular,
as hinted by their blankly cheery faces,
which you wouldn't expect around here.
Once finished our warming Irish cream
we step outside politely saying goodbye
into the hamlet crystallized in silence.
All has gone completely dark now,
were it not for a lamp on the pub's facade
illuminating a sign that reads *to let.*

STARDUSTLING
After Günter Grass

You jump into the world out of the blue,
maybe through some spacetime wormhole,
like any other petty stardust gurgitation.
You are promptly told that all you see
is there for you to catch and hold,
so – as soon as you rise up from on all fours –
you set off to walk the whole extent of it,
duly assured and happily unaware.
Nobody ever says a word
about the boldness and the guts,
the stamina and the nerve,
or what else it takes to stand the course.
That is entirely up to you to learn along the way –
but quick enough to be allowed to choose your end,
or just delude yourself you are –
including spotting jackals in the bushes,
checking vultures overhead,
smelling poisoned watering places ...
namely digging every sort you come across.
Till you determine how the extremely close
and the immensely remote are bound together,
inasmuch as all things and thingamajigs
consist of one and only substance.
Then you will finally be able to pick out
from the cacophonous background chaos
the luringly omnipresent call of stars.

MARE NOSTRUM

The sun still rises from the Dardanelles,
draws an arc to Africa
and sets upon the Pillars of Hercules,
while the eagle has ceased to sweep the surge,
does not fly from end to end anymore.

Sunken down the shoals
off the French Riviera,
hulks of warships act as treasure chests
to the thrill of blue-eyed divers
from outside the acknowledged world.

Someplace around Byzantium,
forlorn in the dark of a crypt
under layers of later erections,
the gold insignia Odoacer shipped to Zeno
await retrieval and upholding.

Looked-after by zealous Italic sitters,
ebony-skinned children
of well-to-do Germanic families
gather colored pebbles on the shingles
of Capri's exclusive inlets.

On the sand of deserted beaches
along the Gulf of Taranto,
captive in the spirals of fossilized shells,
the trumpet of Hannibal's exhausted elephants
reechoes through the millennia.

DARK AGES

Ranging within the two stone dams
encasing Upper Derwent Reservoir.
Towers and walls as imposing
as early Norman keeps
across the vied-for country had to appear.
As sudden as déjà vu,
the morbid, hazardous impulse
to run lost in the forest
besieging the fern-covered slopes
along the shoreline,
or sink in the cobalt blue waters.
For a moment I seemed
to hear clangs in the distance,
maybe roaming gangs of Saxons and Danes
opposing the late invaders,
in the brave but worthless struggle
not to relinquish power
and submit to the newcomers' rule.
Thrill and terror mixing in my blood,
the urge of present days
out of the echo of distant times.
A shiver through the undergrowth
and there I am:
back alone onto the bumpy, winding road
outlined by larches.
Just wind and shadows after me,
bend round bend on end.
Whispers from the flanking shrubs ahead:
disbanding warlord ghosts attend.

CULLODEN MOOR

At last they met. No sound. Arrays deployed.
It was the perfect day – no haze, no shine.
Long minutes lapsed before the bagpipes trilled.

By noon it all ran smooth. Forlorn and void.
No banner waved. No circle stood. No line.
With peace and level smoke the field was filled.

THE EXPEDITION

In the orange gleam
preceding sunrise,
toward bosky hills
shielding the coast,
dew collecting on the skin.

Chasing the lighthouse
by the fortress where the Hero of Two Worlds
called to load more arms and disembark some men,
brave and keen on dying for the making of a country,
yet unwilling to fight for the sake of a king.

A brief pause on Capo d'Uomo,
enough to take a pensive look
at the smoothest sea between Giglio and Montecristo,
before withdrawing through Bengodi
across the former marshland of Maremma.

Anointed with the smell of pines and oleanders,
heavy paces beat the time
to the fast-advancing morning,
while the silver bay reawakens slowly to life.
Once again I've made it back a perfect stranger.

ANOTHER SOUTHERN HISTORY

In the former Kingdom of the Two Sicilies
still the seas are more turquoise,
the skies are bluer,
the folks are more affable,
the speed at which time elapses is lower
than in the rest of the *Bel Paese* –
whatever the advocates of the House of Savoy
or a plethora of mean and hypocritical paladins
of the sordid republic that superseded it may say.
The locals keep solid memories of either's many abuses.
Throughout these long-abandoned lands and waters,
nevermore reconsigned to democracy and progress,
many still regret the enlightened iron hand of the Bourbons,
while some'd even prefer the infamous Blackshirts to return.
They all despise and curse the Hero of Two Worlds,
who never gave a damn about the fate of any people
but always led his horse and aimed his saber
simply where he'd grab the bigger loot and wages.
It was partisan historians who bestowed upon him glories.
He expected none nor ever asked for any of his bloody feats
to be written down in chronicles as something else.

PASUBIO 1915-1918

Expectant sleepers man the crest,
a crag for post, a chink to rest.

They make of heights their firm terrain,
as silence, stillness, blankness reign.

No glint, no plume they watch out for,
don't guess a name for what's in store.

And whom grenades or slugs won't kill,
their poisoned souls or Jack Frost will.

REMEMBRANCE DAY

The shine of clanging helmets rips the weft of space,
the beat of glossy boots disrupts the flow of time.

The cruelest aliens failed to crush the human race,
although mankind had long before betrayed itself.

By millions slighted cries accrete to dazing roar,
until once more they all dissolve to distant moan.

The sun will keep on rising on the darkest hour,
and never will vibrations wane to utter nil.

THE TREES

Amid the hazy country, looking for the marks
of winter. Ice abides the ditches still, but all
the snow is gone. A hobbling, fickle wind, ablow
without conviction, tries to make its presence heard.
A few gray herons, crows and mews are all that sets
the silver background into casual motion. Bare,
majestic trees aligned along the frosty fields
are all that tells the weeks are running by although
the year appears to be appeased, diseased, released
from duties, freed from target dates to meet and ways
to go. As if it had been atomized or fused,
then scattered over dull, unlabeled weather. This,
and more, the sundry, lonely trees narrate. For sure
they are the only ones that know. The steady trees.
They need no clues, no routes, no bearings. None at all.

ALBATROSS

Six months have gone.
He waits, attentive but calm,
despite the shortening of days,
displays austere, assured aplomb,
the most deeply inquiring eyes,
the most elegant avian form.
Beauty made perfection.

When all seems lost,
near the end of the summer,
there she is again, at last, expectant,
circling off the cliff, in front of his hideout,
eager to accomplish the ancient rite.
Life travels on and on, ever,
just to come full circle.

THE THORN

It's still daytime when she's about to prune the roses,
but the long shadows that precede the hug of twilight,
unnoticed, are already taking possession of the ground.
Quick! For the season is well on, the summer draws near
with its swelter, its scalding breath, its unremitting glare.
Clips precise and clean, from the cut stems no teardrops,
only mute whispers through her parched, half-open lips.
The work is soon done to perfection, with no hesitation.
She averts her eyes from the roses for just a split second
and the innocent thorn digs into her reprehensible palm.
Globules of blood drip on the pale-gray leaves, slip down
and streak the rosy petals below, strive to adhere to them
before re-collecting on the edge, then come off and alight.
The thirstiness is gone, the bush healed, the sorrow freed.
And there! The evening has slopped all over the orchard –
the secreted sting is the token, the thorn has been broken.

DOWN THE HOMESTRETCH

It's next to
impossible to know beforehand
whether tears or a smile will come more naturally
the exact moment when – the green days long gone and
the gold ones speeding away – one feels like turning back to
watch the distance covered, contemplate it, rejoice about the
pace having never been too fast, regret it hasn't been slow
enough. And the dust raised all along – still hovering –
impedes one's sight: it's no use straining the eyes,
one had better desist, forget, look
forward.

Thus there
will be no turmoil when – finally facing
the mirror at the end of the course, beyond which
nothing and everything coincide, the brown days down to
fumes as well – in the eyes glossy with disenchantment both
the winner and the loser can be seen. By force of habit one will
shrug one's shoulders, drop one's gaze, take one more step –
the final one – as if it were just one out of millions, unless
the very first indeed. No one will even deign to say
goodbye or leave a note – that's all
there is to it.

A RUNNER'S OBSERVATIONS

Magpies always go in twos,
as one inspects the grass the other keeps a lookout,
nothing has them split for long.

Hedgehogs rather slink alone,
they cross the pavement either way too late or early,
ending up astray or squashed.

Wood frogs hop around in swarms,
they little care if any's left behind or taken,
all that matters is the whole.

People never give a damn,
if many, some, a few or quite the proper number,
each presumes to be the one.

A JOURNEY

Simple living favors simple leaving.

Obviously that wasn't any day, and
neither was she looking forward to some
special one: her dreams had gone at sunrise.
Still, she'd woken up to darker mornings.

Chiming in.

Well-folded clothes, an open case and scent
of rain throughout the clearing shade laid bare
the truth: no room allowed for second thoughts.
A small delay? No way! The glow leaked in.

Embrightened winters stem from conscious falls.

IF ONE DAY
To Jane

Your last breath, awake,
flows into my eternal sigh;
your eyelids, soon to yield,
secure my window open wide.

And while you dream of us
as having always been together,
the dark lights up,
our little room dilates,
I travel through the depths of time
and see ourselves so far ahead –
yet close, forever one.

Then here is what I further view:
even if one day we chanced
around these very parts
in completely different forms,
say – you a doe to rove the woods
and I the wind to blow the dells –
we would abide until we joined anew.

You would hasten hilltop-bound,
looking for a sign;
I would linger all around,
wrapping you as mine.

THE ENDLESS TRUDGE

And there you find yourself, anew, up early in the morning, thinly breathing
in thick air. Blotted-visioned, miry-thoughted, sullied-souled.
The last night's good intentions pell-mell thrown
on the heap of still-searing distant
memories, the lifetime's
seething ones
precipitated
into still
regrets.
Tired-eyed
for the contrast
of shade and shafts of
sunlight filtering through the
French shutters, all ears on the hiss and
bubble from the moka pot. Nothing adventured yet
and nothing ever secured, nothing but the same old inconclusive
hesitation before setting out across uncharted wastes. Forgotten in the dark,
unwinded, disregarded, the clock. Leftovers staling in a dish upon
the armrest. A pen, uncapped, over a notebook open on
blank pages. Maculae, from a past surviving the
present, aglow on the wall behind the
curtains. Blurred days long
gone against the
sharp edge
of a day
barely born
and then already
grown too old. Drowsy
frenzy, hectic torpor, prostrating
awareness. All that's been driven again and
again nonetheless waiting to be met somewhere ahead. The
windows finally open wide. The coffee gone cold once more. Plenty
of untrod road to give in to in the unremitting heat wave. Dearth of footsteps.

CALL

Atop again –
still.
Facing west –
cuddled by the evening breeze.
Commanding
the heart-stopping Pennine extent.
The sun through high, thin, opalescent clouds,
setting in a finally familiar sky.
No thoughts, no more struggle.
No sound,
save that of the air in and out of the nostrils
and the barely audible roar
of a tractor up the slope a mile away.
One more minute
breathing in deeply,
then some buried childhood prayer
dug out prior to running back.

SOLO RUN

Alone in the fog,
amid the faded countryside.

No signs of movement
a furlong all around.

Unbroken silence,
then caws of distant crows.

THE WEATHER TENDER

No word had come through in years.
The mirror does not lie.
The summer of life
had been creasing his face.
So fiercely.
More storms than sunshine.
Sudden. Violent. Fast.
Too sly to anticipate,
unthinkable to tame.
Still, it seemed there could be time
to ponder, attune.
To readjust, make up.
When the first drizzle arrived,
gentle but continuous,
he knew there would have been no going,
either forward or back.
Until longer showers supervened.
Black squalls. And hail.
Then the slantest, weakest rays. And rime.
Days edged on one by another.
Shorter and shorter.
Ever more dozeful. Not doleful.
Neat. Soft. Quiet.
Assuaging.
At last no mark,
not the slightest scratch,
could be found on his skin anymore.
As bright and smooth as never before.
Like the land covered in fresh snow,
like the silent mirror's pane.

GLANCES OFF THE SILL

All those dogged hours
adding up to years.
The bulk of life
before the very same window,
defying the rule of time.
Watching people walk by,
seasons change,
birds fly.
Unseeing anything indeed.
It used to be like a job,
and it used to be fun –
a visual rocking chair of sorts.
The chair's still there,
but the rocking's gone,
and also either kind of words,
the spoken and the untold,
appear to have dissolved.
All is absence now,
but murky remnants
vaguely shifting in the distance
whither they will yet be lost.
Out of mind's control,
above emotions,
beyond physical boundaries,
even past belief.
Just within awareness.
Pupils drained from staring vainly,
a messy mass of emptied eyefuls.
Loose would-be recollections.
Glances off the sill.

BY THE DINING ROOM'S DOOR WINDOW
To mom

What happens in the world
to her is of no interest anymore.
The TV screen is always blank,
newspapers have been piling up
unopened in a nook for quite some time.
She much prefers to spend her hours
by the dining room's door window,
watching mornings, noons and evenings
come and go while daylight's getting longer
and appears to carry back familiar views
to hold on to when shadows lengthen,
such as could allow her mind to bind
both near and distant memories
before they slip away for good.
Because when autumn tempests rage
the wind blows near just doubts
as blowing over sureties one by one.
And in the end some winter comes
that brings along appeasing storms
to gather each and all of them
and firmly bury everything
in thickly falling snow.

BUNGLER

I used to find my time
to stop, take breath, sit down and see,
before we all forgot how life should be.

I lack awareness now,
of why I act the way I do,
as if there were no but, no what, no who.

We charge about each day
and throw ourselves like dice are cast,
despite all futures are to make one past.

CANDY STEALERS

Atonement nights and rejoicing mornings.
As when, still milk-toothed and bruised-kneed kids,
we woke up with a start after unintelligible nightmares.
We used to steal candies from the jar, time from sleep,
sunbeams from the sky, happiness from tomorrow.
Only, now a sigh, though true and deep, is not enough
to erase the darkness of hours on awakening
and the roughness of years at bedtime.
We nurse atonement for interminable instants,
until it dozes off how little suffices to let us recover
our breath awhile, for it's never fast asleep.
We burn rejoicing over a hectic moment,
hopelessly incapable of making a fire out of it,
and its light scarcely illuminates our faces,
like that of a match whose stick runs shorter every day.
In the beginning we didn't care in the least,
later we became more and more concerned,
at present we know for sure, we must return it all:
time, sunbeams, happiness.
Just the candies we're allowed to keep.

BLUE DAHLIA

It's always been about
all that recalls him just,
and us all remaining:
a withered dahlia stem
in a jar on a sill at the back;
the do-it-yourself doghouse
peeling in a darkened room;
the camo ripstop poncho
still hanging in the hall.
A truly modest tomb.

It's funny pictures,
mostly black and white,
lined on dusty shelves;
and paltry fishing prizes,
made of hooks and bobs,
along with other types
too knotty and odd to tell.
One hurried crazy ride
forever on the edge.
A promise hard to sell.

THE PAINTER'S HOLE

On top of the staircase on the northern wing,
as cold as an after-snowfall cloudless dawn –
the unlit landing,
untrodden for who knows how long.

Inside the only flat, still upright on easels
or hanging on moldy walls by jute twine knots –
canvasses and boards,
unfinished, peppered with dead midges.

Smell of greasy dust and spirituous stuffiness,
of dried oil paints and frugal leftovers gone bad –
the whole place laced with the fumes
of tobacco galore and lustra of solitude.

UP TO VAL VENTINA
For Bigio, Moncio, Cindu and many others ...

Hello, good pals of mine too soon gone by!
I seem to hear your chuckle
echo mid the drops of rain
still trickling from the larches,
down remotely swooshing torrents,
over my unrhythmic footfalls.
At first I had hoped I would have met you
further up, across the silent basin,
where the meadows nearly touch the glaciers.
Yet I'm happy that you wished to stay with me
from the beginning of the mule track
all along the lone ascent.
At last I'm pretty sure:
whenever I return to this alpine recess,
beneath unshaking peaks,
fatigued moraines, erratic snowfields –
either trudging or apace,
and even on the run –
I can encounter cheerful friends of old
I would no longer chance upon
in any other place,
as well as former selves –
the child, the boy, the younger man –
elsewhere dissolved and never coming back.
Thereat no stranger may intrude or have a say.

PETALS

For Pier, whom I met just once

A flower is a whole.

Petals are the most fragile
and beautiful of its parts.

Sometimes one falls off,
there is no cold or drought to blame.

It simply happens
to be blown away in a gust.

The flower suffers,
may even seem about to wither.

Until the petals left brace up,
stretch out and fill the gap.

New sap flows up through the stem
into a reblooming flower.

The whole exceeds the parts,
there is more than single petals.

It is one corolla instead,
so that no petal is ever really lost.

And a calyx supporting it,
and the stem supporting the calyx.

And earth supporting all of it.

WHAT'S BECOME OF THE PEANUT-EYED SNOWMAN?

Paper, pastels, slate and chalk.
May hay and August corn.
Sweat, soap and talcum powder.
Carrot and potato soup.
Scents from the age of daydream,
as neat as four decades ago.

Almost all the rest has disappeared,
gone blank and mute within the tangle,
except for a vermilion streak below the knee
and wild screams across the schoolyard.
Where is the stately elm
that used to tower at the center of our realm?
The iron roundabout? The secret hideaway?
What's become of the peanut-eyed snowman?
Who's taken his straw hat and besom?

How discordant to have to travel over a thousand miles
to come to grips with such a sulk, to feel at ease,
free and brave enough to take such backward leaps!

One of the remotest cutbacks goes like this:
Say, Do, Kiss, Letter or Will?
A kiss on her freckled cheek, without a word,
I would have liked my sole reply to be.
Say, however, is just what I would always say.
Remember is my only choice today.

THE DAMNED ONES

They're impeccable peers
indeed – at bottom selfless,
polite, sociable and candid.

The thing is – it is not ours
to question why – nobody
ever trusts them one iota.

It so happens that sweet
violets end up weeded out
as if they were thorn apples.

That's the nub of it – scent
is taken for stink, goodwill
for malignant intrusiveness.

There are no longer ears to
listen or eyes to watch – just
to hear and see insensibly.

Kindness is totally missed,
when not openly despised for
the ubiquitous want of it.

They're easy targets for scorn
and contempt – souls simply too
big for the room left in heaven.

SKYCE

The moment you discover I'm not there
and fail to find whatever trail I've left,
don't think I have turned tail or let you down.

To get in touch with what I'll be anew
you'll have to leave your cozy flatland home,
be heading north until the ground slopes up.

Once reached the dell you'll have to cross the bridge
and take the track that ends where giants rest,
then scan the line uniting sky and ice.

THE SECRET OF ARCHERY

Most have it
that they trace their course,
set their targets,
decide when and where
to aim the arrow.
A tiny few realize
that others string the bow,
then nock and draw it –
so hard a fact to accept.
All grow old
buying or fantasizing
they're the masters of their lives,
and they go on and on,
convinced it is themselves
that set and keep them going.
Once gone that far,
nobody can stop them
or turn them away from their mark.
They know no love, no hate,
nothing at all;
they have no real will,
no wishes, hopes, scruples, regrets,
insight, first or second thoughts.
They're not the brain in this,
they're not the eye,
they're not the hand,
they're not the bow,
they're not the string.
Yes – they are the arrow.
And the wait, the wait ...
the wait once drawn,
while shaking in tension,
is wearing them out

more than the fear of missing.
But much less than the one
of never being released.

ACKNOWLEDGMENTS

Nearly all the poems in this collection, at times in slightly different versions, have first appeared or are forthcoming in the following journals:

Acumen, Carillon, Dream Catcher, The Journal, Jupiter, The Interpreter's House, Iota, The New Writer, Orbis, Other Poetry in the UK;

Artemis, California Quarterly, Chiron Review, The Clarion Review, Hawai'i Pacific Review, Italian Americana, Light, The Lyric, Main Street Rag, Möbius, Poetica Magazine, Red Earth Review, San Pedro River Review, Sanskrit, Santa Clara Review, The Society Of Classical Poets' Journal, Songs Of Eretz, Star*Line, Tipton Poetry Journal, The Weekly Avocet, The Worcester Review, World Literature Today in the USA;

Poetry Salzburg Review in Austria;

Existere, The Nashwaak Review in Canada;

Paris/Atlantic in France;

Contemporary Literary Review India, Phenomenal Literature in India;

La Ballata, La Clessidra in Italy;

Poetry New Zealand in New Zealand;

Carapace, New Coin, New Contrast in South Africa.

I am deeply grateful to my wife Jane, my first reader and devoted editor, especially for putting up with my pedantry and linguistic obsessions.